Because, It's Just Good Manners!

For more information, or to place an order, please contact:

Fine Images Printing & Copying
6342 NW 18th Drive, Unit #6
Gainesville, FL 32653
http://www.fineimages.me/
fineimages@cox.net

Publisher:

Columbia County PC Incorporated
PO Box 3473
Lake City, FL 32056
http://columbiacountypc.org/
clc@columbiacountypc.org

This book was printed in the United States of America.

T' is a subtle reminder of the simple things we have all but forgotten!

Janet Horton, Author

Because, It's Just Good Manners!

Because, It's Just Good Manners!

It is a fact; we are a society that judges based on performance and appearance. We judge people, and are judged by others. Knowing this, we still do not look at ourselves through the eyes of others or note how our performance is seen by others.

We are quick to judge and therefore, quick to be judged. Sometimes we find ourselves in new circumstances or situations that are uncomfortable and we do not know how to act so, we "open mouth and insert foot". You have all heard that saying, as well as others, such as "Do unto others, as you would have done to you."

This book is not about lecturing – though I may do that a little.

Sometimes we need to sit back and remember "it's just about good manners and common courtesies".
Every day we face situations in which we should be showing, just by reflex and habit, common courtesy. We are so conditioned today, that we no longer even expect or anticipate being treated with good manners.

Basically, if you consider the other person first,

you will do fine. Think of it as reverse psychology or selfishness. What goes around comes around so, if you are courteous to others, they will be courteous to you – therefore, you benefit.

We are not talking formalities. If what you say and do is hurtful or invasive to others, or causes you have second thoughts, you have probably erred. If you feel the compulsion to explain your actions or make excuses, then you know you did wrong.

Put yourself in the other person's shoes and be honest with your assessment. If you find the actions hurtful, offensive, or objectionable, they probably are. When you find yourself laughing at the expense of another person, it is probably not a good thing. This is not about snobbery, good breeding or acceptable society behavior.

Good manners and courtesies apply everywhere - school, home, work, church, and on the street. If you are a leader, a supervisor, or someone admired, do you want to be remembered as the rude jerk? The lack of good manners and common courtesies are also recognized as abusive and bullying behavior. Regardless of your age, those are labels you should not be comfortable with.

Here is another important distinction. Good manners, and common courtesies, have nothing to do with respect or trust. Everyone is entitled to good manners, and common courtesies, even you. However, trust and respect are earned.

People who earn trust and respect will also have, and practice every day, basic good manners and common courtesies. Trust will earn respect. Respect will earn trust. Trust and respect are found in good leaders, ethical, reliable, and dependable persons with good communication skills, and people confident in their knowledge and actions.

Knowing good manners and common courtesies is a learned way of life. Someone has to teach you verbally, by the written form, or by example. Otherwise, you never learn. If your parents do not know, they will not be able to teach you or set the example. However, that is no excuse for you not to learn.

Anyone can set an example, including a younger person for an older or elder person. Surprise someone every day, by showing a little common courtesy and good manner.

The opinions and suggestions found in these pages are strictly mine. After being born into an abusive family and having survived abusive relationships, I did break the cycle. With determination and a strong will power anyone can break the cycle and walk away from abuse.

Now, let us get down to basics.

Contents

Introduction

1. Greetings ----------------------------------- 1
2. Door Etiquette ------------------------------ 5
3. Cellular Telephone ------------------------ 6
4. At Home ------------------------------------- 8
5. In The Bathroom -------------------------- 10
6. Conflicting Morales ---------------------- 11
7. Living on the Defense -------------------- 16
8. Internet and Email ----------------------- 22
9. Personal Values -------------------------- 24
10. Public Behavior -------------------------- 30
11. Road rage ---------------------------------- 32
12. Smoking ------------------------------------ 35
13. Social behavior -------------------------- 37
14. Table manners ---------------------------- 42
15. Work Courtesies ------------------------- 46

In Summary ------------------------------------- 49

1.   Greetings

Why does the idea of greeting someone make us uncomfortable? Is it pure embarrassment because we don't want to be the only one, or don't remember the name? Get over it. Think about it! Don't you feel better when you have been greeted, even if it is a simple "Good Morning" or "Hi"?

When you can, refer to the person's name. Use it as a form of recognition. If you don't remember the person's name but recognize their face, simply own up to it. Would you feel embarrassed or uncomfortable if someone walked up to you and said "you look familiar? I know I should know you, but I can't remember your name"?

Remember, that takes guts and confidence. Do you want to be remembered as the person with the guts and confidence, or the shy coward? Don't get excited. The only difference between the two is that the shy person hasn't asked the question yet. After you have asked the question a time or two, you get more confident and realize it is not a big deal.

When you walk into a room, elevator, or office, simply say Good Morning or Good Afternoon or whatever is appropriate. People appreciate being recognized and acknowledged. When you are in a room and someone comes in, does not acknowledge you, do you feel snubbed, ignored, treated rudely?

When you walk into a room and say "Good Morning Ms. Smith", do your buddies laugh? Are you embarrassed? Don't be. They are probably laughing because they are embarrassed because they were rude and now know it. Turn the situation around and communicate on their level. Say, "What's the big deal, just say hello?"

You played down the situation, showed confidence, and they will now probably follow your example.

Now the loaded question, you come into a room, and it is full of people, who do you greet first? Common sense will give you this answer but we typically over think things and talk ourselves out of the obvious. It is always the woman before the man. If your parents are in the room, they come first, in my book. Next, would be your host or hostess. After that, you start with the oldest - or eldest, and work your way down. Keep in mind, that depending on the circumstances or the event, you will not necessarily be expected to greet everyone in a room.

Don't interrupt conversations or cause awkward situations. You can always approach the individual later, or the greeting may not be necessary. Stand quietly to the side and if the person does not acknowledge you within a moment or two, move on to someone else.

Keep the level and tone of your voice conversational. If you have to raise your voice, you are trying to accomplish something in an inappropriate environment.

I am not sure where the age break is so let us suffice it to say that if the person is from a later generation than you that makes that person your "elder". Do not greet them by first name, unless they have given you permission. By the same token, everyone is entitled to the Ma'am, Sir, or other title that sets them apart from others, such as Uncle or Aunt.

Elders are special people. They have been around longer and accumulated a degree of wisdom not yet realized by the younger set. They have a level of maturity that can only come with age. Like everyone else, they are entitled to good manners and common courtesy.

Don't ask those questions that you would not want to answer. You may think it funny to embarrass the person, but imagine you in their shoes, and you are the one embarrassed? Do not ask humiliating questions or make comments on a person's appearance. Just because, in your opinion they dressed in poor taste, doesn't give you the right to act in bad taste.

When you are ready to leave, it is always appropriate to say Good Night - or similar greeting - to your host.

Anytime you bring a guest into someone's home, or to any social event, you always introduce them to the host. When you bring guests into your parent's home, you show them the courtesy of being introduced to your friends. It is their home and their business. Your parents, or your host, are accountable for the people on their property.

When you greet someone with a nod, a verbal hello, or a handshake, remember to smile. That smile can really light up a person's face and tells them the greeting was sincere.

2.   Door Etiquette

When you are entering or exiting a building, and you see that someone is right behind you, hold the door open for them.

If you are near a door and see someone approaching, open the door for the person.

When you see someone approaching a door and their hands are full, offer to assist them by opening a door, or help by carrying a box or package.

In the situation where a building as more than one set of entry doors, open the first door, hold it until someone else can take hold of that door, and then open the second set of doors and hold that door open until everyone has had a chance to enter.

Elevators are big issues and cause a lot of confusion. It is polite for the man to enter first, to assure the elevator is safe, before allowing a woman to enter. The man is first on and last off so the door can be held.

Whether it is a man or women, always offer to open or hold the door. It cost little to display good manners and courtesies.

3.   Cellular Telephone

Cellular telephone usage is now the vain of our existence.

The use of cellular phones or conversations on cellular phones is supposed to be private and confidential - even when you don't think so or care. The rest of the world is not interested in your private business, and the person you are talking to, may also be offended by your lack of privacy and consideration. Is it appropriate to talk about family business in public, or company business in public? Never!

Seriously, the rest of the world does not want to hear your private telephone conversations and the person on the other end of the telephone will appreciate the privacy.

It is also irritating to have a meeting or event constantly interrupted by a ringing, buzzing or vibrating telephone. You may think you are being considerate by putting the phone on vibrate, but you are still interrupting the occasion every time it hums and you get up to take the call.

When you are driving, with other people, standing in line, in a restaurant, or anywhere else, with anyone else, you should not be answering or on the telephone. We are talking seriously rude.

You decide if you want to talk on the phone, or be with other people. Don't be rude by being with other people, then ignoring them, so you can talk, or text, on the telephone.

When you are driving, never take the call, unless you are able to pull off the road.

Everyone is entitled to "alone" time. Mine is from 9PM until 9AM. People over the years have learned that about me and do not call during those times. The land line is open for emergencies and the cellular is turned off.

Let the answering machine or voice mail take the call. You can always call back.

4.   At Home

This is really where we take good manners and people for granted.

When you are expecting company, it is always polite to at least offer a beverage. Granted, when your buddies drop in you may suggest they "help themselves" to drinks in the refrigerator. From that point on, when they come over, they will expect to repeat the privilege. Adults are more inclined to remember their place and recognize that fine "familiarity" line that should not be crossed.

You can kindly accept or decline the offer. If you are a regular guest, you could offer to help serve, and help clean up afterwards.

It really isn't polite to just drop in on people. They have a life and so do you. How would you feel if there was something you really wanted to do, and there was an unexpected knock on the door? Now, reverse that. How inconsiderate and rude do you see the behavior now?

Never continue to watch television, talk on the telephone, surf the internet, or work, when you have company. When you are in someone's home, by invitation, you expect to be given their undivided attention - they deserve the same thing from you.

When you have music playing in the background, turn it down. If people have to compete with the music in order to have a conversation, then the music is too loud.

On those occasions when people are sleeping or ill, keep the sound down to a minimum. This is especially difficult when there are people around that are hearing impaired however, solutions are also at hand - they are called headsets.

Have you noticed the difference in the way you treat company or guests in your home versus how you treat family? When you have a guest, you are polite, ask them what they want to watch on television, offer them a beverage, carry their dirty dishes to the sink, etc. Yet, you never show those same courtesies to your family. Why?

When you are with a group watching a movie or television program, do not talk while the movie is showing or the television program is being broadcasted.

5.   In The Bathroom

Bathroom etiquette is a must and very private area.

Clean up behind yourself.

Do not hog the bathroom.

Do not use other people's toiletries.

By all means, flush the toilet.

Respect other's need for privacy and do not go barging in.

Put your dirty clothes away and hang wet items to dry. Do not leave the room looking as if a hurricane stopped in.

Men, put the seat down when you are finished.

Remember to close the lid when finished.

6. Conflicting Ethics

Conflicting ethics or morality will always suffer and be an issue between generations. Certain issues have and will remain points of contention or dissension. It is hard to think about this or think of the future, but in the back of your mind, there has to be the thought, do I want to do something that will come back and haunt me someday.

Depending on the country, the family, religion, and the laws, the answer here will never please everyone. However, with that said, there has to be a place to draw the line, regardless of the age of the individuals involved.

Is it okay to greet someone in public with a hug, handshake, and quick kiss? Yes, with qualification. Not everyone is touchy-feely and will always take exception to any kind of affection, in private or in public.

Obviously, lengthy kisses and situations where arms and legs are wrapped around individuals are behavior that is more appropriate behind closed doors.

If it can be embarrassing or offense to others, then the general code of good manners and courtesy come into play. You will always run across people who deliberately attempt to offend or embarrass others without any regard for the hurt or pain they are causing. This is generally referred to as negative, destructive behavior, and in some countries subject to arrest for exhibitionism.

When you feel the need to sneak or perform, your instinct is already telling you that your actions are inappropriate.

Like it or not, but we are judged by the way we act and dress. You do it to others, and others do it to you. Consequently, when you wear little or nothing and expose a great deal of skin, you are sending a message, and it may not be the one you intend. The way you dress is a form of speech. If you do not want to be misunderstood, be careful what you say - how you dress.

Young people are brutal with their name calling and teasing. Just because you think something, it does not mean you have to say it – especially if it will be hurtful to someone.

When you want to be perceived or treated as a professional, you have to dress for the part in life that you want to play.

Violence, under no circumstances, in any form, should ever be tolerated. Abuse or bullying behavior is found in men and women, children, and white collar as well as blue collar workers. It can be in the form of nitpicking and nagging, to negative feedback. Verbal abuse can be as psychologically damaging as physical abuse. When you tell someone they will never amount to anything, over a period of years, they become brain washed into believing it.

You can find almost all forms of abuse in the average, typical, home. It is taken for granted and not even realized. It comes in the form of intimidation, threats, ultimatums, leverage, and discipline, yelling, and using each other for punching bags. People casually slap, or punch someone, without even thinking of the perception. You witness children having a fit and throwing things at each other without any reaction from adults.

On a playground at school, you see one child throw a ball at another child - just a little too hard but no one does or says anything about it.

Students watch teachers embarrass students and nothing is ever said or done about it.

Students, bully students, and nothing is done about it.

In the workplace, you find rude abusive

behavior even in the form of the infamous cold shoulder.

We encounter rage on the roads and walking down the streets. People, regardless of age, no longer feel a need to control their violent tendencies. When a parent is driving down the road, with children in the car, and the parent is yelling out the window at other drivers, a clear message is being sent to the children.

Violence is never acceptable and yet we have learned to turn a blind eye to the events. It isn't that we do not see. We are actually embarrassed by the display. However, when nothing is done to the adult, or child, to correct the actions, the message is clear - it is okay to be abusive. Violence is acceptable behavior. It is okay to be a bully.

That is not to say we should never discipline. However, we have to consider the appropriate time, place, and manner, and it has to be for the correct reason. In public where sensibilities can be affected, and where people can be embarrassed or humiliated is never the right time or place.

We also see an unfortunate trend in schools across the country where violence and unsportsmanlike conduct are becoming the norm by students, faculty and parents. Parents have a responsibility to promote decent and competitive behavior, in the home. Traits used at home, or in the family environment, will be used outside the home. Anger management and violent tendency must be recognized by fellow students, faculty, and parents, and dealt with.

For every parent, there is a story to tell about bad behavior by a child, and for every child, you will probably find a story to tell about an abusive parent. The cycle repeats and reoccurs.

7.   Living on the Defense

Defensive living is the same as being in a situation that is out of control. That is never a good situation, and all the common sense in the world, seems to leave our mind.

Masculinity, integrity, and hurt feelings are bad influences. Each is serious and we will fight for them, but when we fight, aren't we doing just the opposite of our intent?

Think about it. If you are being put in a defensive mode, you are probably being pushed by someone who feels threatened by your masculinity or integrity. So, to respond, defeats the position you are already in.

The other side of the coin is that you did make a mistake, and need to own up to it, and be done with it.

Hurt feelings can never be defended. You let yourself be vulnerable, and you got hurt. That was your choice, your bad. Take it as a lesson learned and move on.

A girlfriend or boyfriend that cheats on you, was not really your significant other, were they? Chalk it up as a lesson, remember the good times, and move on.

Try to step back and look at the situation factually and objectively. Deflate the situation quickly, and honestly before it gets out of control. Remember that emotions and principles never win in a disagreement or conflict. It takes courage to live by your convictions and to be able to separate convictions from emotional highs and lows.

There are a few reasons why or how people end up in positions of control. One is that the individual has proven themselves and earned the trust and respect of others, so they have put the individual into the position of control. It has been earned.

Another is from lack of confidence, self-worth and self-esteem. If you have the remote control or are driving the car, people have to watch what you want, or go where you take them.

If there is a family outing, and you do not go, then you are punishing the family - you think. Surely, they will have a miserable time without you.

You constantly defend yourself and your actions. You bully and verbally or even physically abuse others that do not bend to your demands and insults. What is that all about? Do not expect your family and friends to understand if you do not reach out to them.

The idea of failure, or of being worthless, or useless, is completely and totally demoralizing and debilitating, and it is extremely embarrassing to talk about. People who do not share those feelings simply do not understand, cannot be empathetic or sympathetic.

There are all kinds of objective ways to look at these situations, and you definitely have the advantage because you have already identified that you are different. The question here is, are you different in a bad way? No, because there is no such thing. Why can't being different, be a good thing?

Next, consider that some, if not all of your symptoms are due to a medical condition and even depression? Oh I know, there is a terrible stigma attached to being depressed, and the doctors always want to load you down with drugs, but that does not mean that is what will happen to you.

Sometimes, the reality is simply a state of mind. If you do not know what to do with you, or your self-worth, why would anyone else? It is not the world's responsibility to figure out where you fit in. It is your job to find your niche. You might be objective, logical, methodical, and therefore, very talented - just not acknowledged. You feel backward, introvert, and lack social skills. You probably get bullied a lot because you are different.

You may even stand out simply because of your ethnic background, your sexual preference, or religious beliefs. Who cares? Others are defensive or antagonistic because they do not understand. That is their problem. You are who you are, and what you are, and you believe what you believe.

Because of you insecurities you may strive for control and be antagonistic. Understand why you are being the way you are, and work your way out of it, because it is destructive.

There is a psych project that doctors love to put people through that works. It is hard and painful but in the end, it really does pay off. No matter your age, you can do this throughout your life because it is always a reality check - attitude adjuster.

It exists under several names, and the column headings change but the principle is always the same. You have two columns or pieces of paper. On one sheet, list all your accomplishments and I mean all of them. It doesn't matter how trivial they are. Even if you just helped a little old lady cross the street, write it down. Do you know what that one comment tells about you?

It tells that you are aware of your surroundings - you are observant. You did an act of kindness. You showed good manners.

Let's try another example. You completed your homework or completed a task at work. Your instinct might be to ignore that because you were getting paid to complete the task or was required to. Wrong! By completing the task, it proves you are methodical, logical, a problem solver, that you have the ability to follow-through and to meet deadlines.

Each accomplishment can be explained and appreciated. Now, the other sheet of paper is the shortcomings or liabilities. This we usually have no difficulty in completing because we are so easily self-critical.

Remember, these are the shortcomings that you can identify, not accusations people have made against you. Your parents may scold you because you never clean your room, or your boss may get on your case about always being late to work, but they do not know the underlying cause. You do.

The point is, the more you know about yourself, the more you understand your need for control, and the more you will be able to let go of that control.

This is a roundabout way of say you might start acting like a bully because you lack self-confidence for no real or life altering reason.

8. Internet and Email

The internet and email are such a major part of our day to day life that we can't overlook the courtesies that go along with it.

Never, type your email and online documents in all caps. That is the equivalency to cursing someone out or yelling at them.

Remember there is nothing private about a computer - email or online so don't type or send something that you do not want the public to be privy to.

Computers are very personal and contain personal and private information. If it is not your personal property, leave it alone.

Do not hook on to someone else's internet service.

Do not install someone else's software on your computer. Another important thing to remember, when it comes to a computer, your worst enemies are your friends, family, neighbors and co-workers. Everyone claims to know more than you - and they may when it comes to their computer. However, when they really mess your system up, they will almost never offer to pay to get it fixed.

Email should be short and simple - focus on one topic per email.

Don't use cutsie terminology or emoticons. Your paragraphs and messages should make sense and not be open to misunderstanding.

Always reread your email on content and context and run a spell check program.

Use an appropriate subject line. It should be two or three keywords about the content or intent of the email.

Be sure and sign your email. If you require a reply instruct the recipient how you want to be contacted.

Does the email have a point - a purpose? Is that purpose made clear?

Watch your language - no slurs or cursing. Be cautious of any negative comments about other people.

9.   Personal Values

Personal values are just that - personal, and they define everything there is about you. It is similar to your own signature, fingerprint or footprint. Your personal values are the foundation to your sense of good and bad, or right and wrong.

Personal values are developed as you observe, read and learn, as you grow and experience life. These are not genetically inherent or necessarily a by-product of the society we live in. The values we established will affect every aspect of our life: our education, health, religion and spirituality, integrity and loyalty, career, wealth, stability and security, and creativity.

As you age, and mature, you rely upon the example of others, your own common sense, and your gut instinct. Do not be bullied or intimidated into situations that go against every grain of intuition you have. Your value system is strictly yours, and you should not have to defend them. If you feel a need to defend them, then they are not really yours.

As you build that sound, deep and strong foundation on which to build your life, people will see the courteous, calm, confident, generous, broad-minded, tolerant, and talented person you are. You will become that person who is a good listener and not feel threatened by new concepts, lifestyles or ideas, and appreciate the limitations of each of your values.

Values are valuable and have value. You do not have the right to pass judgment on another person's values, and vice versus. If you need to confront someone, wait until the timing is correct and the emotional environment can be controlled.

Make your point in a way that no one's dignity is destroyed, values are not attacked, and embarrassment is not an issuc. Whether this is between family, friends, or strangers, this is a fact to be lived by.

Values result in character traits that may stem from awe to disgust to frightening and amusing. Character traits are attributes, such as habits, and displayed attitudes, and qualities that people will use to judge and stereotype you. These traits identify your distinct personality and set you apart from others who see your playfulness, seriousness, interests, awkwardness, etc.

Through your values and traits, you become

who you are and those things influence all aspects of your personality, your physical appearance, your social habits, and how people identify with you. Essentially, you have developed a personality - a reputation by which you will be known.

As you build these values and traits - this personality, this reputation, you develop confidence. You build courage, the courage to live by your values and convictions. Your thoughts and opinions are yours, and you are comfortable with them. You no longer feel the need to justify, explain or defend. You become calmer, more self-assured. However, courage is more than that. It becomes the confidence - the ability to do what needs to be done in difficult times.

Be leery of negative personality traits or flaws as well because they work to balance with the positive traits. A negative trait may be a desire or ability to cause hurt or harm to another or have a negative affect other people, their livelihoods, their health, their safety or even their moods to a point you could pose a risk to society and need medical assistance.

Peer pressure is when we accept a certain way of living, dressing, talking, socializing and even thinking because we want to belong and gain approval. If we cannot belong to the best group or gain their approval it is even more important not to gain their disapproval.

Disapproval results in bullying, ridicule, and peer humiliation. To be set aside by fellow students or co-workers is the ultimate rejection and painful. The bulk of our day can be spent in demoralizing surroundings day in and day out where people are insensitive and blunt in their criticism.

Young people say what is on their mind, without any censoring, caution or thought, when they notice different behavior. It doesn't matter that the difference is financial, the manner of dress, or way of life.

Young people also emulate adults who are quick to judge and criticize different lifestyles, ethnic backgrounds, and religious beliefs they are not familiar with. Like sponges, people – young and old alike - watch and learn from behavioral traits and then practice the jealousy, selfishness, anger, and the acting out.

These are prime examples of bad manners, crude behavior, and ignorance. This type of peer pressure can be hurtful and scar a child for life, or at least have long term impact well into adulthood. Adults are supposed to nurture and teach by example the better parts of ourselves.

You cannot win in a battle against close-mindedness, narrow-mindedness, discrimination, bias, or prejudice. It is the unknown that threatens these individuals and results in their defensive and bullying behavior. There is no explanation, justification, or logic, they can offer to support their position or why they feel threatened by you.

Your peace does not come from whether you wear your pants with the crotch down at your knees, but, from your values - from within. Your peace does not come from their approval or disapproval because, to be approved or disapproved, will be a battle against your values.

If you have to work at approval or disapproval, it is probably not the right group for you. Take your time, the right group will find you - or vice versus.

When you encounter someone in your life who displays negative character flaws, it is better to avoid these people.

Watch your carriage - walk straight, use good standing and sitting posture. Remember, the way you look, act and sound is a form of communication. Don't slap or touch someone on the arm every time you want their attention. Do not laugh loud enough to distract or disrupt the room.

Dress for the occasion - appropriately for the event or place.

Make it a habit to use correct grammar and pronounce your words to the best of your ability. If you find people are constantly asking you to repeat yourself, don't get defensive, there is a reason you are not understood. Deal with it.

Be humble - always put others before you - except in line, then you do not have to let people in front of you, unless you really want to.

Do not hold up lines chitchatting with people.

Be prideful and proud of who you are because you are a person of value.

10.   Public Behavior

Is it ever proper to discipline someone in public? No. Whether it is a child or another adult, you can always take the individual aside or outside or to another location. It is embarrassing and humiliating for everyone – the on-lookers and the people involved.

Is yelling at children across a store a good thing? Certainly not and is actually teaching the child it is acceptable behavior.

Is it acceptable behavior to allow a child to scream and run around unsupervised in a restaurant or store? Certainly not! It represents a disruption and interruption to everyone and a hazard to others as well as a liability for the place of business.

 If the child is not ready to conduct himself with reasonable good manners, then the child should not be in public. If the child is too tired to behave, then take the child home. If the child is spoilt and wants to have a hissy fit or is accustomed to throwing tantrums to get their way, then take the child home.

Never touch a person, their property, or their children without permission.

Never discuss money with people.

Do not talk on your cellular phone while in line.

Watch your language so that you do not talk offensively while in public.

Do not slur people by name, religion, and the way they appear or by ethics.

You should never cut in line or push people out of your way.

Never stare at people or listen into their private conversations.

When you need to move ahead or through people, always say "excuse me".

11.   Road rage

Road rage has become a major concern on our highways.

Do not tailgate.

Use your turn signal when changing lanes or turning.

Do not cut or weave in and out of traffic.

Have everyone in the vehicle use seatbelts.

Don't yell at people out of your car window because they did something that irritated you. Some people are just oblivious to everything that is going on around them and to their own bad manners.

Driving requires your undivided attention and concentration. Under certain conditions you are not driving in a safe manner and putting other drivers and your passengers at risk.

Do not talk on the cell phone while driving.

Do not eat and drive at the same time.

Do not play with your pet while driving.

Do not hold back traffic. Get out of the way, change lanes. Pay attention to the speed limit and the traffic flow. When you need to get out of the way – then get out of the way, safely.

Stop at stop signs - do not roll through the stop. Stop means stop. That means to come to a complete standstill with no movement. You move forward when it is your turn to move forward or the way is clear.

Yield at yield signs - do not stop if no cars are coming. Yield means to merge in with incoming traffic. You stop, only when there is a flow of traffic and you have to wait for an opportunity to merge in.

If you cut in or cut someone off, you are going to end up making someone mad. Remember how you react when you cut someone off.

Stop at red lights and yellow lights, go on green lights. Do not accelerate through a light or floor the accelerator when a light changes.

Leave the horn alone - it is for emergencies, not for anger.

Do not be a backseat (passenger seat) driver.

Do not drink and drive or partake of any drugs,

prescription or otherwise.

Drive the speed limit.

Check your blind spots and use your mirrors
before attempting to change lanes or turn.

When you are approaching entrance ramps,
move over a lane to allow incoming traffic to
flow into traffic. Not everyone understands the
principles of merging and will not yield to you
so do the courteous thing and get out of their
way.

Drive defensively, not offensively. You may
believe you are a good driver but you do not own
the roadway or control the other drivers. Good
manners and common courtesies are critical on
our highways. They could save your life.

Do not block driveways or street intersections.

Do not drive toward someone with your high
beams on.

12.   Smoking

Smoking is a sensitive subject but needs to be included.

When other people are around, before you light up, asked if anyone minds if you smoke. There could be medical reasons why a person cannot or should not be around cigarette or cigar smoke. Ask before you cause harm to another individual.

Certainly never smoke in someone's home or vehicle without their permission.

When you do smoke in another person's home, use an ashtray and empty the ashtray when you are finished.

Don't discard cigarette or cigar buts in their yard or flowerbeds.

Keep in mind that when people have said "no smoking" the terms or extent need to be clarified.

People that do not have a tolerance for smoking or cigarette smoking for personal, medical, or environmental reasons are usually vocal about their personal values and feelings. Regardless of their reasoning, remember that cigarette smoke is carried on clothing, skin and hair. You may resist a cigarette for a few minutes, but the smoke is still there and doing hard.

When you have someone in your home and you know they have issues with smoking, you can resist the urge to smoke, but remember the smoke is already in your furniture, the walls and draperies.

As a courtesy, when you invite someone into your home you need to advise them that smokers live there. This is your preference and chosen lifestyle, not their choice.

Remember, their values are their values, just as your values are yours.

It is a difference of opinion or lifestyle, and not the end of the world.

When someone invites you into their home for a social or service event, and you are a non-smoker, you have an obligation to yourself to tell the person your conditions.

It is just good manners to make your guest comfortable, within reason.

13.   Social behavior

Social behavior is something we overlook, should not, and take for granted.

Always stand when a national anthem, of any country, is being played.

Show courtesy to all flags and religious symbols.

You may not appreciate, support or understand a country's philosophy or politics, but someone does and a lot of people have sacrificed their life for those beliefs. If you believe strongly in something, love someone, or pattern your life based on a belief, how would you feel if dishonor was shown?

Never forget to say thank you, no thank you, excuse me, or please. It is a small point, but much appreciate. We forget to say these words and yet appreciate hearing them, and they carry unbelievable weight and importance.

It doesn't matter if it is the property that belongs to a co-worker, sibling or family member, respect that it is their property - not your property.

Don't violate another person's need for, and

entitlement, to privacy. You would not want anyone taking your property or violating your privacy. When you violate privacy or take property, no matter how small, from someone else, you immediately and automatically cause them to go into the defense mode.

This includes items in which a person has spoken for, but not yet claimed. If you know it, do not cross the line. If you borrow something, take it back. If you break something, repair or replace it. Be considerate toward others.

Remember everyone else does not have the responsibility of cleaning up after you. It is common courtesy to clean up when you finish. To ignore these responsibilities only puts you in a potential abusive situation.

Do not interrupt conversations. Wait until it is your turn, or you do not have food in your mouth.

Watch your language at all times. Cursing and slurs are not acceptable language and can be hurtful to others.

Younger people may be a little more energetic that adults but either way, there is acceptable public behavior, and it does not include rowdy, loud behavior.

Don't crowd a sidewalk or walkway and yield to other people. When someone steps aside for you, say thank you, nod, or wave to them.

Say "excuse me" when you need to cut through a group or crowd.

Look both ways before you step off the curb. Your lack of caution could cause a driver to over react to a potential danger.

Watch how you handle your umbrella because you could accidentally stab someone or dump water on them.

When you are at work or school, and you use the kitchen or bathroom, clean up behind yourself. Don't use other people's property or supplies, put the dirty/wet items away and wash and dry the dishes. Don't sample someone else's toothpaste, cologne, perfume, or shampoo.

Take out the trash after you have contributed smelling items to it.

When you leave a room, turn off the light.

When you are finished with the television, computer, or radio, turn them off.

Do not slam the doors as you come and go.

After you have done the laundry, be sure to remove all your clothing from the washer and dryer, and all the lint from the catchers. Do not use other people's laundry supplies without their permission. If you are doing the laundry at home, okay, but if you are using a public facility, never leave your laundry unattended.

Incidentally, there is nothing worse than a person who always mooches off other people. Pay your own way.

Do not bring children to an adult event or get together.

Take your hat off when you are indoors.

Do not wear sun glasses when you are inside or having a conversation with someone - it is rude. People want to see your eyes.

Do not point or stare at people. It makes them uncomfortable - wouldn't you be?

Do not make fun of people who make mistakes. It could be you.

When someone is talking to you - look them in the eye and give them your undivided attention.

When you are dependent upon others, do not keep them waiting and always thank them. If you are being picked up or dropped off, offer to pay for gas.

If someone does you a favor or invites you into their home, return the favor or invitation.

When you invite a person out, and you choose the restaurant, it is traditional that you pay the tab. At the time of you extend the invitation, you should make this clear, so there are no misunderstandings at the restaurant.

Do not - never - loan people your credit card or money.

Always ask questions, be modest, and let others talk about themselves.

When walking down the street with a female, men always walk on the street side - women on the inside.

Never shout across a room or raise your voice when talking with someone.

Give a wide berth when pushing a stroller or shopping cart so that you do not run into people or block the way.

14.   Table manners

Table manners are where common mistakes are made. Typically, this is another area in which we are guilty of just not thinking.

Seriously, why are these things important? The next time you are in a restaurant or cafeteria, look around. Do you want to be the person remembered for sitting up and looking confident - or the person slouching in his chair, dropping food down the front of his shirt or her blouse?

Do you want to be the person remembered because he talked with food in his mouth and dripping down the corners of his mouth or spitting food on people as he talked?

Do you want to be the person not able to enjoy his meal because the person sitting next to you has their elbows on the table, essentially squeezing you off the table?

Do you want people to perceive you as a "beggar" or starving because you slump over your plate and cram food into your mouth as if you have not seen food in a month?

Eventually, we all have to learn to eat with a knife and fork and know when to use them.

When we see someone pick up a piece of meat, such as a steak or pork chop, and proceed to eat with their hands, we turn away and accept or "assume", they never learned to eat with a knife and fork or did not have access to the proper eating tools. It is crude and we are embarrassed.

When you are properly dressed, and you sit down at the table, you conduct yourself in a more mature way than if you came in your underwear or pjs right out of bed. You get what you pay for - as the saying goes. If you want to be half-hearted about having a meal at the table, then maybe you will get half a meal.

Many times we get lazy and begin to take our meals in front of the television and even on television trays. What we are learning is how not to sit at the table properly and how to conduct ourselves while at the table. You can carry that casual, lazy, demeanor with you when you go into a public restaurant, with friends and family, and then be truly embarrassed.

Not only is it polite to offer a lady a chair but equally polite to assist her with it. Some women may have a tendency to display their independence - under the veil of women's rights and equality - and take exception to you helping with their chair. That's okay. It is the good

manners that count. Always ask if you can
assist. The lady can always say no.

Using the proper tableware really does make
eating more pleasant. Remember the knife is
for cutting and the fork is for putting the food in
your mouth.

Basic good manners at the table also mean
passing food, rather than grabbing and throwing
items across the table.

Certain traits are completely unacceptable,
such as blowing your nose at the table. Excuse
yourself from the table and seek privacy. Not
only are those activities rude, they are
offensive.

Remember, when actions result in
embarrassment, someone is going to respond
defensively.

When you eat, do not slurp or drink your soup
out of the bowl.

Do not burp at the table - or make other
offensive noises. Unfortunately, parents have a
tendency to teach children this crude behavior
is cute and they continue the behavior in public.
It becomes an embarrassment to the children
and parents – who do not or apparently to not

know any better, and to the people around them.

Place your napkin on your lap.

If there is a hostess, or host, wait for that person to start before you begin to eat.

When the other people at the table prefer to start the meal after saying grace or observing a religious ritual, wait until they start eating and sit respectfully in the meantime.

Take small bites and chew quietly and with your mouth closed.

When dining out, the man should order for the woman and himself, if it is a social outing. This is an indication of a personal relationship and a courtesy extended to that partner.

Children should be seen, and not heard. They should not be permitted to crawl around over and under the table or the other eaters.

Children should not be permitted to disturb the other guests or patrons.

15. Work Courtesies

Work courtesies are rarely extended and taken for granted, which is a serious error.

When you use the staff room or kitchen, clean up after yourself, and do not use other people's supplies and property.

Do not borrow from co-workers or lend to co-workers.

Get to work on time - be punctual.

Return phone calls, emails and voice mail in a timely fashion.

Business is business - the workplace is not the place to play around.

When you jamb a machine, clear it so it is ready for others to use.

When you use the last of the supplies, see they are replaced. When you take the last of the toilet paper, put a new roll on the spindle.

When you take the last cup of coffee, make a fresh pot.

Greet your co-workers every day - with a smile

on your face.

Watch your posture, show your confidence.

Keep your word, meet your commitments.

Offer to help others.

Look the part - dress accordingly. If you want people to take you seriously then you have to take yourself serious. Remember the way you look is a form of expression. If people are getting the wrong impression, is it because you are giving the wrong impression?

Watch your language - no cursing and do not make negative comments about your co-workers.

Do not gossip.

Janet Horton